OCS Study
MMS 2001-065

The Deep Sea Gulf of Mexico:
An Overview and Guide

Inhabitants of the Cold, Dark, and Food-Limited Deep
Gulf Show Adaptations for Crushing Pressure
and the Ability to Subsist on the Gentle Rain of
Organic Particles from Above

U.S. Department of the Interior
Minerals Management Service
Gulf of Mexico OCS Region

OCS Study
MMS 2001-065

The Deep Sea Gulf of Mexico: An Overview And Guide

Authors

Benny J. Gallaway
John G. Cole
Larry R. Martin

Prepared Under Purchase Order #17037

By

LGL Ecological Research Associates, Inc.
1410 Cavitt Street
Bryan, Texas 77801

A deep sea crab, *Rochinia crassa*. Long appendages are considered by some as a deep sea adaptation to prevent sinking into soft oozes.

Published by

U.S. Department of the Interior
Minerals Management Service
Gulf of Mexico OCS Region

DISCLAIMER

This report was prepared under a purchase order from the Minerals Management Service (MMS) to LGL Ecological Research Associates, Inc. This report has been technically reviewed by the MMS and approved for publication. Approval does not signify that contents necessarily reflect the views and policies of the Service, nor does mention of trade names or commercial products constitute endorsement or recommendation for use. It is, however, exempt from review and compliance with MMS editorial standards.

NOTE

Unless otherwise noted, all photographs in this document and the companion CD-ROM were taken by Gregory S. Boland as part of the Northern Gulf of Mexico Slope Study, Contract 14-12-0001-30212.

REPORT AVAILABILITY

Extra copies of this report and an indexed CD ROM containing all photographs in this report may be obtained from the Public Information Office (Mail Stop 5034) at the following address:

U.S. Department of the Interior
Minerals Management Service
Gulf of Mexico OCS Region
Public Information Office (MS 5034)
1201 Elmwood Park Boulevard
New Orleans, Louisiana 70123-2394
Telephone Numbers: (504) 736-2519
1-800-200-GULF

CITATION

This study should be cited as:

Gallaway, B.J., J.G. Cole, and L.R. Martin. 2001. The deep sea Gulf of Mexico: an overview and guide. U.S. Department of the Interior, Minerals Management Service, Gulf of Mexico OCS Region, New Orleans, LA. OCS Study MMS 2001-065. 27 pp.

The Deep Sea Gulf of Mexico: An Overview and Guide

Benny J. Gallaway, John G. Cole, and Larry R. Martin
LGL Ecological Research Associates, Inc.

INTRODUCTION

The Gulf of Mexico—sunbathing on sandy beaches, swimming and surfing, deep-sea fishing, red snapper, reefs and oil platforms, SCUBA diving, shrimp dinners. These are but a few of the word associations and mental images that come to mind with the mention of this natural resource. Many are aware that this habitat supports the Nation's most valuable commercial (shrimp) and recreational (red snapper) fisheries, as well as provides nearly 95 percent of the Nation's total offshore petroleum production. Nearshore Gulf habitats and their creatures have been featured in the scientific literature, in magazines, and on television documentaries and sporting shows for decades. On a relative basis, the nearshore Gulf habitat is well understood and appreciated by scientists and laypersons alike.

However, it is only the shallow margins of the Gulf of Mexico that are really understood and appreciated by the lay public and, indeed, many scientists. Mention the Continental Slope of the Gulf and few mental images are invoked. What it looks like, what species live there, and why and how they live there do not readily come to mind. When the Continental Slope is discussed, "deep sea" takes on a whole new meaning—from 600 to 10,000 feet versus the 100 to 300 feet normally thought of as deep-water by most laypersons. Yet, it is the Continental Slope habitat of the Gulf where vast new petroleum reserves have been discovered, and the technology is in place to develop these reserves. The question becomes "Are we ready for this development?" That is, "Do we know enough to estimate the effects of the development on the deep-sea environment?" A common misconception is that we know little or nothing about the slope environment and biota. This is far from the truth.

The Bureau of Land Management, whose offshore responsibilities devolved upon the Minerals Management Service (MMS) almost 20 years ago, recognized the need for ecosystem information about the Continental Slope over two decades ago. First, they commissioned a renowned deep-sea ecologist, Dr. Willis Pequegnat, who had conducted extensive research in this system, to compile all the known information about this Gulf habitat. Drawing upon the results of this study, published in 1983, MMS next designed and contracted a multi-million dollar research program to LGL Ecological Research Associates, Inc. and Texas A&M University to study this habitat during the period 1983 to 1987. The objective of this multifaceted program was to develop a basic knowledge of the deep Gulf fauna and their relationship with their environment.

Geographically, the study extended from the eastern to the western Gulf and focused on habitats and biota living in waters on the order of 1,000 to nearly 10,000 feet deep. The study employed (1) standard methodologies to measure water temperature, salinity, and dissolved oxygen from the surface to the bottom; (2) box corers to take mud samples and biota living in the mud from the bottom; (3) trawls to capture larger animals cruising along and above the bottom; and (4) deep-sea camera systems to take photographs of the bottom and the associated animals and signs of animal presence (tracks, trails, burrows) recorded in the

sediments. Extensive chemical analyses were conducted on water, mud, and animal tissue samples. Later in the study, additional sampling was conducted by using manned submersibles to better investigate newly discovered patches of large tubeworms, mussel beds, and clam beds scattered across the slope in proximity to hydrocarbons seeping out of the bottom.

The results of the study were presented in four annual reports, with the Year 3 and Year 4 reports providing the final analyses. These two final reports included over 2,000 pages describing the program and its results. Known as the "Northern Gulf of Mexico Continental Slope Study" (NGMCS), this investigation provided the first synoptic view of a

virtually pristine deep Gulf. Selected overview data from this study were published in the formal scientific literature, and the data and specimens continue to be used even today by scientists and by graduate students preparing dissertations and theses.

Never, however, has a nontechnical summary of this investigative effort been provided for managers and laypersons. Benthic photographic sampling of the bottom during the NGMCS obtained about 48,000 images of the deep Gulf. These images can be used to provide visual characterizations of the seabed and the resident biota of the deep Gulf. These images have been catalogued by sampling location and depth, and were again reviewed to extract

representative images of the bottom and the resident animals large enough to be seen in photographs. Our goal is to provide a clear perception and understanding of what the deep Gulf really looks like, and a description of the major environmental factors that govern the shape and look of the picture.

SETTING THE STAGE—A PRIMER ON THE DEEP

The Gulf of Mexico, sometimes called America's Sea, covers an area of more than 1.5 million square miles, and at its deepest it is over 12,000 feet, or more than 2 miles, to the bottom! The Gulf is virtually enclosed by the landmasses of the United States, Mexico, and Cuba. The submerged margins of

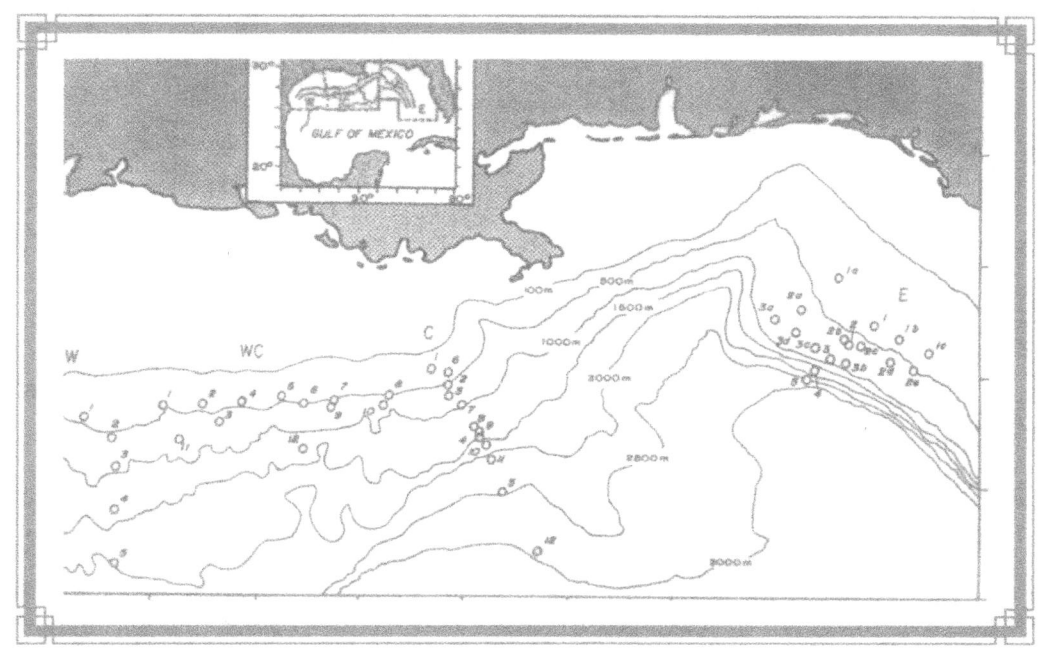

The Northern Gulf of Mexico Continental Slope Study sampled 46 different areas at depths ranging from slightly less than 1,000 feet (300 meters) to nearly 10,000 feet (about 3,000 meters).

the Gulf are bounded by a relatively shallow and flat continental shelf (from the shore to a depth of about 600 feet), which can be quite broad in some places (for example offshore west Florida, Texas-Louisiana, and Campeche) and narrowly restricted in other places (such as near the mouth of the Mississippi River and offshore eastern Mexico). At the shelf break, the seafloor begins to slope steeply towards the abyssal plain of the deep Gulf, often terminating in a near-vertical scarp or cliff-like formation that extends on down to the bottom. This region is called the continental slope and extends from the shelf edge (600 feet deep) to a depth of nearly 10,000 feet deep. This is the region of interest for this essay.

The Loop Current— Dividing the Gulf

The configuration of the landmasses enclosing the Gulf restricts the size and location of the openings that allow water exchange with adjacent seas. Both the inlet and the outlet are located in the southeast corner of the Gulf basin. Water flows into the Gulf from the Caribbean Sea through a narrow inlet (the Yucatan Channel) situated between the west end of the Yucatan Peninsula and Cuba. The deepest part of this inlet is only 5,000 to 6,000 feet compared to the 12,000 feet in the deepest parts of the Gulf. This flow continues north towards the United States mainland, then loops to the east and bends south along the Florida Peninsula. Water exits the Gulf into the Atlantic Ocean as it flows easterly between the south tip of Florida and Cuba, the so-called Florida Straits. This dominant circulation feature of the Gulf is called the "Loop Current." The northern area of the "loop" often pinches off to form cyclones (counterclockwise circulation) and anti-cyclones (clockwise circulation). These eddies wander along the Continental Slope region of the

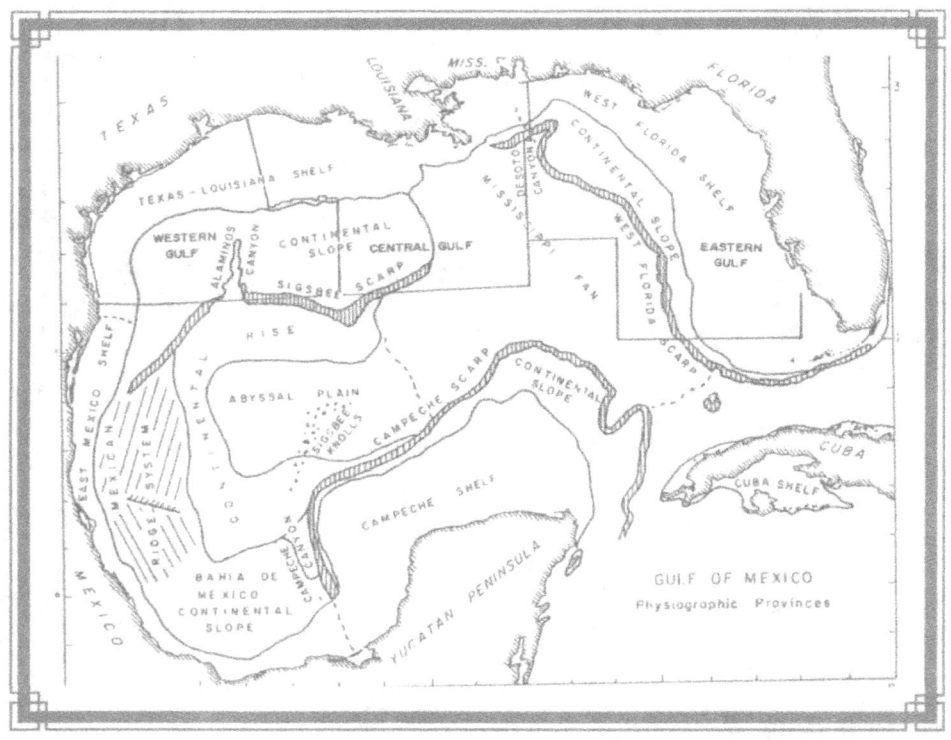

Physiography of submerged land forms in the Gulf of Mexico. The perimeter of the Gulf is ringed by a shallow shelf, seaward of which the seafloor steeply slopes downward to the abyssal plain of the Gulf--the Continental Slope.

Gulf to the west and south, even into the Bay of Campeche, before dissipating.

The Loop Current and its branches drive the major surface circulation of the Gulf and account for some of its biological features. The currents bring pelagic larvae and fishes, plant material, and heat into the eastern Gulf. However, the currents also influence the western Gulf to a lesser degree by spinning off eddies that drift slowly westward. As can be seen, the western Gulf is somewhat isolated from the Loop Current. This "isolation" corresponds to the observation that more species in the western Gulf are restricted to that region alone (that is, they are not distributed Gulfwide) than is the case for eastern Gulf species.

Mississippi River Discharge Important

The second environmental factor that, like the Loop Current, has effects on a massive geographic scale is the Mississippi River. Its waters pour into the middle of the northern Gulf (off the United States mainland) and then spread westward over the continental shelf. Other rivers drain into the Gulf, but their influence is dwarfed by that of the Mississippi River System, which is among a dozen of the great rivers of the world. It delivers about one million cubic yards of sediment and vast quantities of organic material to the Gulf each day. The huge volume of sediment accounts for a building delta and continental shelf to the west.

The mouth of the river is located in a region where the Continental Shelf is very narrow. Consequently, accumulations of sediments are deposited on the shelf edge and may from time to time slump down-slope, devastating the bottom fauna. At the same time, however, these events deliver huge volumes of sediments and organic matter to the lower reaches of the slope where energy or food supply is limited. The huge amount of sedimentation deposited on the slope in the region near the mouth of the river results in a submarine blanket of soft sediments, called the "Mississippi Fan." This feature bisects the northern continental slope of the Gulf, with more typical slope features found to the east and west of this sediment blanket.

Important Physical-Chemical Factors Vary by Depth

A third factor that influences the distribution of slope animals is the presence of vertical layers in the water column. These layers intersect the seabed at various depths and create changes in the physics and chemistry of near-bottom waters. These factors have either direct or indirect effects, or both, on the bottom-dwelling animals. These vertical layers can be characterized by light, temperature, pressure, salinity, and dissolved oxygen.

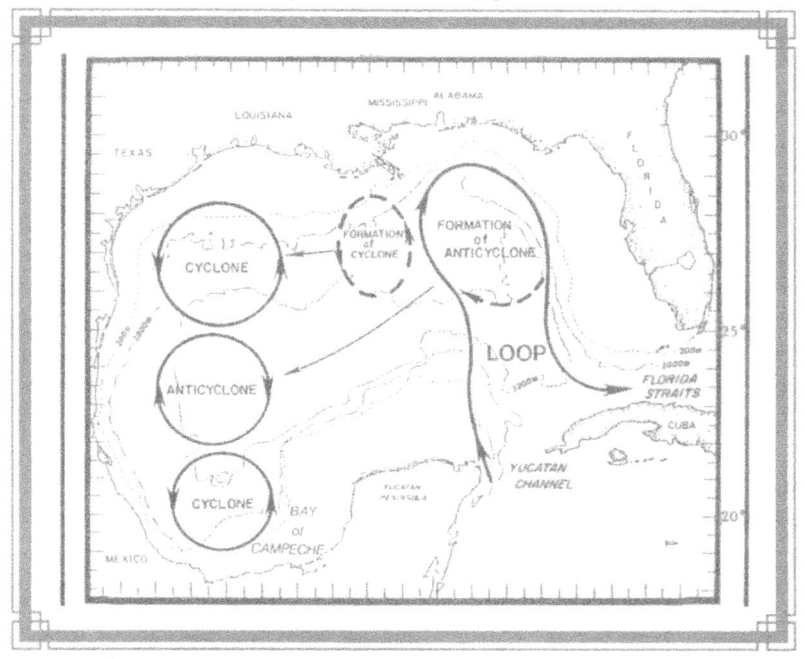

The Loop Current and its associated eddy features (cyclones and anticyclones). Note that both the entrance and exit of the Gulf of Mexico are in the southeastern part of the Gulf.

5

Light is sufficient to allow microscopic plants (phytoplankton) and other plants like seagrasses to convert carbon dioxide to sugars (a process called photosynthesis) usable as food by animals. However, photosynthesis occurs to a maximum depth of only about 200 feet. Thus, the entire slope is below the depth where photosynthesis can occur (the euphotic or "true" light zone). Below 200 feet, twilight conditions, ever darker with depth, persist down to depths of about 3,300 feet or 1,000 meters. Below this depth, darkness prevails year round. The zone between 200 and 3,300 feet is called the "disphotic" zone (limited light). Deeper depths are characterized as "aphotic"; that is, without light.

Surface water temperatures are influenced by sunlight and air temperature. Water temperature declines rapidly with depth down to about 3,300 feet (1,000 meters) where temperatures average about 4 °C (about 39 °F) Gulfwide. From this depth, water temperatures remain uniformly cold down to the bottom. Thus, a succinct characterization of the continental slope is that it is a dark and cold place to live.

Not only that, pressure forces increase nearly linearly with depth. At the surface (one atmosphere) we experience 14.7 pounds of pressure per square inch. There is roughly a one-atmosphere increase in pressure with each additional 33 feet of water depth. Thus, animals at 3,300 feet experience 100 atmospheres of pressure, or 1,470 pounds per square inch on their body surface. At 12,000 feet the pressure is well over 5,000 pounds

per square inch! Thus, one might expect that some special physical adaptations are in order, and that expectation is correct.

Salinity, like temperature, is relatively high at the surface (on average around 36 to 37 parts per thousand [ppt]) and declines with depth, but only by a few parts per thousand (corresponding bottom water salinity would be about 35 ppt). With dissolved oxygen content, however, there is a discrete

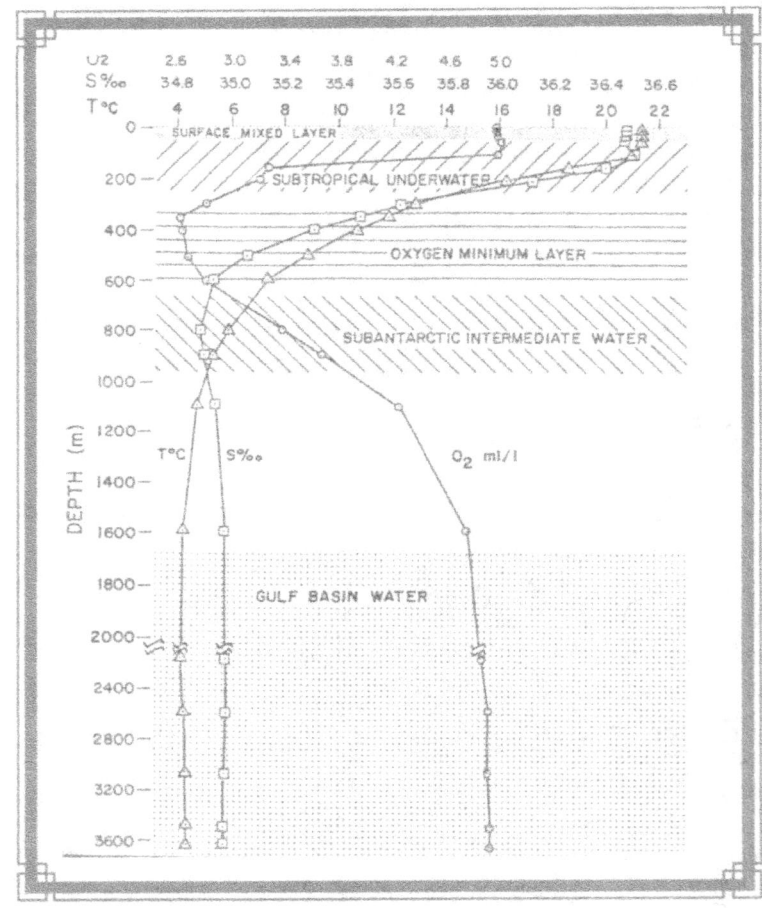

Vertical water layers in the Gulf of Mexico. Note that below 3,300 feet (1,000 meters) the water is uniformly cold (about 4 °C). Further, it is at this level that light totally disappears.

6

oxygen minimum layer that occurs at depths between about 1,000 and 2,000 feet. Where this layer bathes the slope, there is a corresponding zone of high biological standing stocks. The depressed dissolved oxygen concentration might impact some species but not others. Those species that can deal with low oxygen levels are successful. The key point may be that the oxygen levels in this depth zone may not be sufficient to oxidize organic matter as rapidly as elsewhere, making it more accessible to biota as a source of food or energy.

Sediment grain size and the mix of these sizes greatly influence the types of animals that live in the sediments. Sand-sized particles are the largest, followed by silt- and then clay-sized particles, which are the smallest. On the continental slope of the Gulf, silty-clays dominate the bottom, especially at depths below about 1,600 feet. As will be seen later, the visual character of the sediment blanket suggests a tranquil environment in terms of currents, with only a few exceptions. Analysis of over 20 bottom sediment parameters considered important to the benthic fauna showed distinct sediment zones by depth:

shallow (to 1,600 feet), intermediate (1,600 to 6,500 feet), and deep (greater than 6,500 feet).

Limited Food or Energy Sources

With one important exception that will be discussed below, the bottom communities of the deep Gulf live in a food- or energy-limited environment dependent upon production from the surface layers of the Gulf. The solar energy that drives ocean systems is fixed by phytoplankton into chemical energy that is used by animals. This process occurs in the euphotic zone, as we learned above. Much of this plant production is consumed by small grazing animals (called zooplankton) which, in turn, are eaten by larger animals like small fish. Even larger animals feed on these, such that a surface layer (the pelagic zone) food web is established. What is left over, including waste and undigested food material passed through this food web, ultimately sinks through the water column to the bottom. These organic materials can be viewed as an "organic rain" of food to the bottom. Detrital rain from the pelagic system is supplemented by organic detrital material from the landmasses (terrestrial carbon) in areas affected by significant river discharge. In addition to these rains of detrital foods, slumping and

A conceptual model of the Gulf of Mexico Continental Slope. Food for the deep sea comes from surface water production and from river outflow, but only that part that is left over or degraded after being processed by the shallower components of the ecosystem reaches the bottom. The deep Gulf suffers from extreme energy limitation.

erosion of bottom sediments can be a significant means of energy transport from shallow to deeper areas of the bottom. Nevertheless, the deep sea is a food-limited system.

The recipient of this rain (perhaps drizzle would be a better term) is the bottom zone of the deep ocean referred to as the "benthic boundary layer." Biologically, this community consists of the organisms living in or on the sediments, plus the assemblages of animals in the overlying water column immediately above the bottom. Animals living in this part of the water column are said to be "b e n t h o p e l a g i c ." Benthopelagic animals are a subset of the "nekton," swimming animals that live in the water column. The designation of benthopelagic refers to the fact that, although they live in the water column (pelagic), they mainly occupy the waters just above the bottom (benthos).

The sediment community consists of bacteria and small (often very small) invertebrates, above which, at the bottom-water interface, larger animals crawl, ingesting both the sediments and the biota living there as food. Other types of animals attach themselves into the sediment or onto a small rock and filter the water for food particles as these pass by in the current.

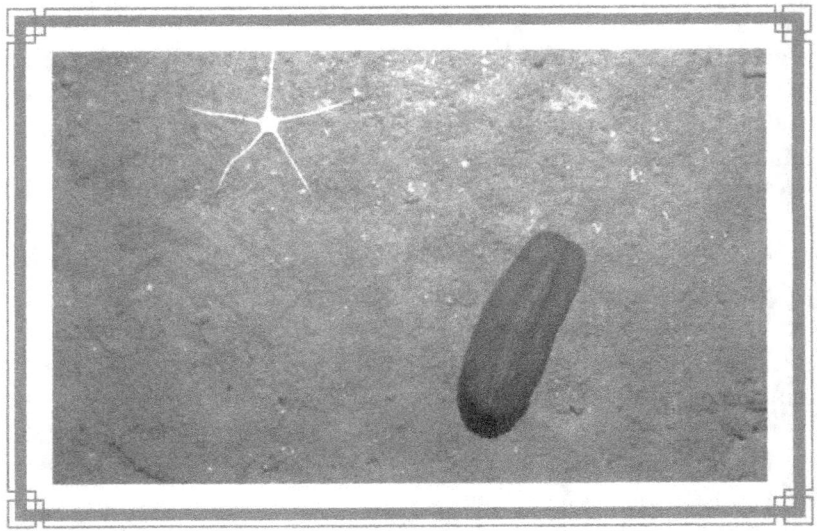

Denizens of the benthic boundary layer, a brittle star, and a colorful sea cucumber. The sea cucumber eats surface sediments and the small animals living in the sediments.

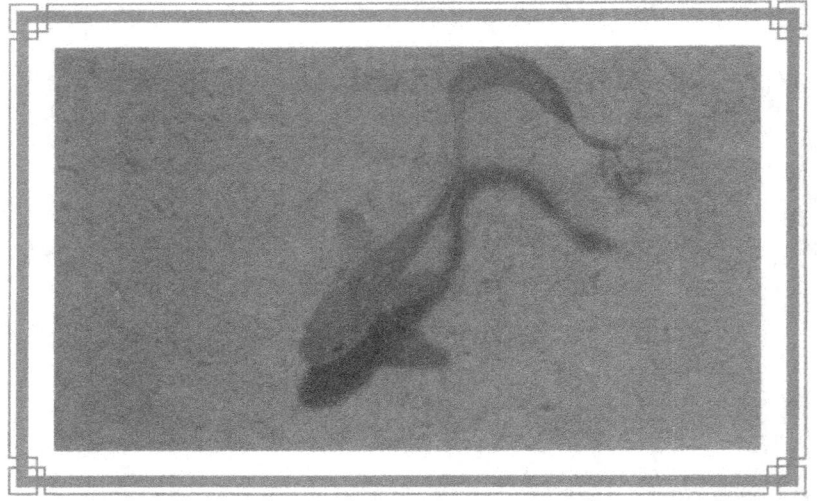

A benthopelagic rat tail fish cruises above the bottom, likely in search of food.

In the water column above the sediment water interface, what we now know as "benthopelagic" fish and invertebrates feed on animals in the water column, as well as those on and in the bottom. Many of these benthopelagic species move up and down the slope bottoms, as well as higher in the water column, to feed, and then return to the bottom. Sediment-dwelling animals also make forays into the water column. Thus, there is an active exchange of food throughout the water column, as well as on and in the bottom sediments. These migrations result in a continuum of communities from the top to the bottom.

From the above descriptions, one can see that the bottom communities of the deep sea occupy an energy-poor environment, with the energy constraints becoming ever more severe with increasing depth and distance from land. This is especially true in the Gulf of Mexico. Primary production in the euphotic zone of the Gulf is not very high, compared with other oceanic areas. Therefore, standing stocks of deep-sea benthic communities in the Gulf would be predicted to be lower than in more productive areas of the world's oceans, and this idea was not discounted by the NGMCS results from the mid- to late-1980's.

The invertebrate communities living in the sediments of the deep Gulf are not very numerous and are very small compared with their shelf counterparts. This leads to low biomass levels and reflects the overall food limitation of the system. However, these animals are very diverse, that is, many, many different species are found. The diversity of this community is as high or higher than diversities characteristic of tropical rain forests, which are usually considered to be the most diverse of planet Earth ecosystems.

The Exception — Chemosynthetic Communities

We have noted above that there is an exception to the food limitation character of the deep sea. So far, we have implied that photosynthesis (conversion of carbon dioxide to sugar by plants using light energy) is the only source of energy to all animals, not counting a few bacteria that can act like plants in this regard. Other than these forms (plants and bacteria), we have suggested that all other animals eat living or dead organic material originally produced and/or derived from plants at the base of the food chain. In 1977, this view of the world changed with what has been classified as one of the major biological discoveries of the century!

This discovery originated in the deep waters of the Pacific Ocean. Using the research submersible *Alvin,* scientists discovered an oasis of densely packed animals, where none was expected, at a depth of over 8,500 feet in the vicinity of a hot, hydrothermal vent laden with hydrogen sulfide. Bacteria in the water around these vents were using carbon dioxide in the presence of oxygen and hydrogen sulfide (instead of light) to fuel the development of sugar. But what was remarkable was that these bacteria were not only living in the water and on the bottom in films or mats, but were also living in the tissues of numerous newly discovered species of giant tubeworms and clams.

A new form of productivity—called chemosynthesis—for animals much larger than bacteria had been discovered to

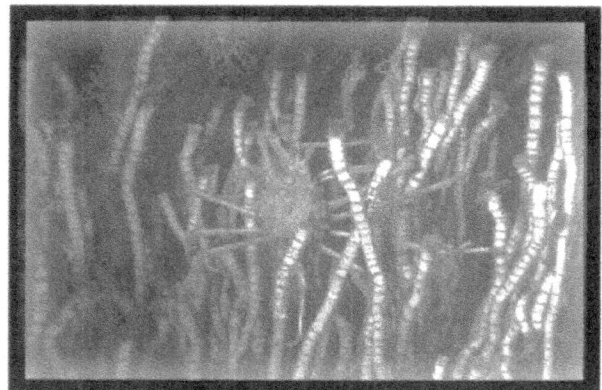

A deep-sea crab crawls in an exotic forest of chemosynthetic tubeworms, which can reach lengths of up to 10 feet. Photo by J. Blair, National Geographic.

A starfish and crabs experience a bonanza of food and shelter provided by a chemosynthetic mussel bed. Photo by J. Blair, National Geographic.

occur in the total absence of sunlight. Chemosynthetic animals were defined as those life forms that are able to live on dissolved gasses through a "symbiotic" (living together for mutual benefit) association with chemosynthetic bacteria living in their tissues. In return for their food, the larger animals provide the bacteria a secure home. Such animals usually occur in densely packed assemblages of large animals over and around the hydrocarbon seeps or vent sites that provide their energy. These clusters of large animals, in turn, attract other life forms like snails, fishes, worms, seastars, shrimp, and crabs, much as a reef in shallow water does. Taken all together, these assemblages form communities that do not depend on the fall of scarce foodstuffs from the surface waters far above. By virtue of the ample nutrient source (the gasses and symbiotic bacteria), chemosynthetic animals of the deep sea have larger average

physical size than the typically small deep-sea animals. The great biomass found at these deep sites is usually hundreds to thousands of times greater than the biomass levels found on the surrounding seafloor. This exception "proves the rule" that nutrition is a limiting factor to the abundance of most animals in the deep sea.

Chemosynthetic communities were documented to occur in the Gulf of Mexico in 1984 around cold seeps, places where hydrogen sulfide and hydrocarbons (mostly methane gas) seep from the bottom. Such communities have been intensively studied since their discovery and are the subject of another MMS nontechnical publication, *Gulf of Mexico Chemosynthetic Communities: A Teacher's Companion*. In summary, Gulf of Mexico chemosynthetic communities are of four types: those dominated by (1) tubeworms, (2) mus-

The first record of chemosynthetic tubeworms in the Central Gulf of Mexico, a photograph from the NGMCS program taken on 12 November 1984.

sels, (3) large clams living on the surface, and (4) small clams living under the surface of the mud. Each of these communities displays distinctive characteristics in terms of how they aggregate, the size of the aggregations, the geological and chemical properties of the habitats in which they occur and, to some degree, the associated "normal" biota that are attracted to and live among them.

The number of known chemosynthetic communities in the Gulf of Mexico now exceeds 50.

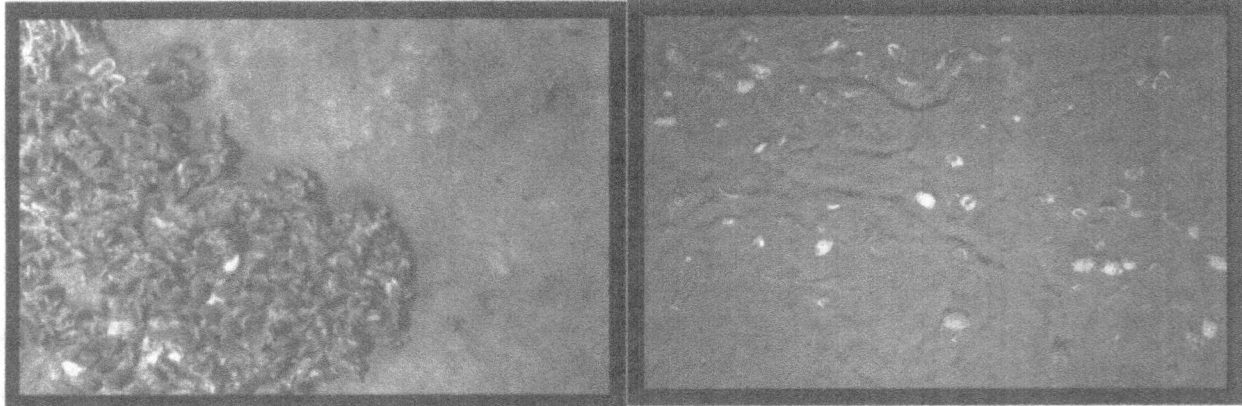

A chemosynthetic mussel bed (left) and a chemosynthetic assemblage of clams (right) living in the vicinity of hydrocarbons seeping from the bottom. Note how sharply defined is the boundary between the mussel bed and the surrounding soft bottom.

No two communities are exactly the same. They reflect locally distinct geochemical microhabitats. Communities can change rapidly over distances of only a few feet. These communities range in depth from less than 1,000 feet to one found at nearly 10,000 feet. Scientists believe that there are likely to be many more, especially in deep water. Natural oil slicks seen at the water's surface in the deep Gulf support this view.

The level of natural oil and gas seepage in the Gulf is surprising. Estimates obtained using photographs taken from space indicate that approximately 10 million gallons of oil per year seep naturally from the bottom of the Gulf. Although released slowly over a very large area, this natural seepage is the equivalent of an *Exxon Valdez* oil spill every year.

Many surface slicks coincide well with known positions of chemosynthetic communities. There are many surface slick locations that have yet to be investigated for the presence of chemosynthetic communities, thus the belief that chemosynthetic communities are more numerous than documented at present. In summary, these rather unusual assemblages are given preferential treatment in the deep Gulf of Mexico. Before operators can develop an area, they are required to submit geophysical survey records that are used to determine that the area is clear of any chemosynthetic communities before development proceeds.

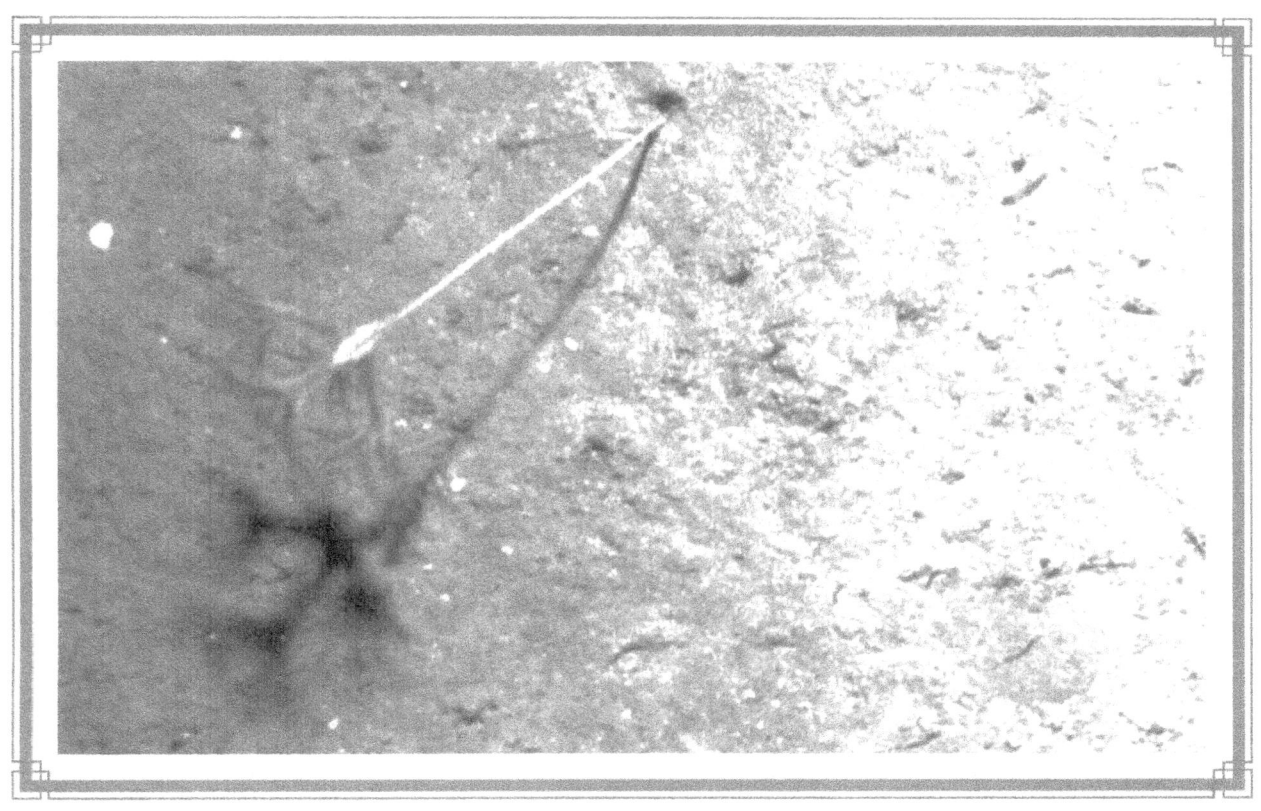

Attached to the bottom, a sea pen filters the overlying water for food.

11

A LOOK
AT THE DEEP

Let us now return to the overwhelmingly larger and massive soft-bottom matrix in which the relatively few and small chemosynthetic communities are imbedded. The photographs here were taken by a camera suspended on a wire from a ship and maintained about 6 feet off the bottom—quite an endeavor considering the bottom was from over 1,000 feet to nearly 10,000 feet below the ship. The camera was equipped with a timer and a strobe light set to take a picture every eight seconds as the ship drifted or motored slowly along a depth contour over a distance of about one to three miles. At a 6-foot altitude above the bottom, the size of the bottom area photographed is a rectangle with one side about 4 feet and the other side a little under 6 feet. The total area depicted by the full photograph is on the order of 25 square feet. A total of 46 different areas were photographed, some on multiple occasions. Overall, 60 camera drops were made using a camera with a standard 28-mm lens, taking 800 photographs per drop (48,000 total images).

The Deep Ocean Bottom

At the time of this study, 17 years after the NGMCS study was initiated, the photographic images are still available for all of the 46

The Benthic Underwater Camera System (BUCS) developed by LGL to investigate the deep Gulf environment.

different locations investigated in the early to mid-1980's. The film rolls from each station were cut into six image-long strips of consecutive frames and these strips were placed in a sleeve holding seven strips. After removing some of the end strips without information (photographs taken as the camera was being raised or lowered), the photographic record for each station was reduced to slightly fewer than 800 images. Those images are now catalogued by location in 17 to 19 numbered sheets, each containing 42 images. We randomly selected 100 six image-long film strips to characterize the bottom for east, west, and central regions of the Gulf that were studied. The only requirement was that each station had to be represented by at least one sample. The 600 images thus selected, except for those with no discernible subject, were scanned onto the CD-ROM that accompanies this report.

From these, we selected representative images to show the visual character of the bottom habitat of the continental slope of the Gulf of Mexico.

Plate 1 shows representative bottom photographs organized by depth and by region across the Gulf from east to west. The series starts at the top with samples taken at about 1,000-foot depths and proceeds down to almost 10,000 feet. One word can be used to describe the visual character of the vast majority of the Gulf of Mexico Continental Slope bottoms—monotonous. The photographs reflect, that on the whole, sediments are fine-grained, and this was confirmed by the grab samples of the bottom taken at these localities. Most of the sediments occupying the bottom are in the silty-clay size range (that is, small or fine-grained), with only slight regional depth variation in the proportions

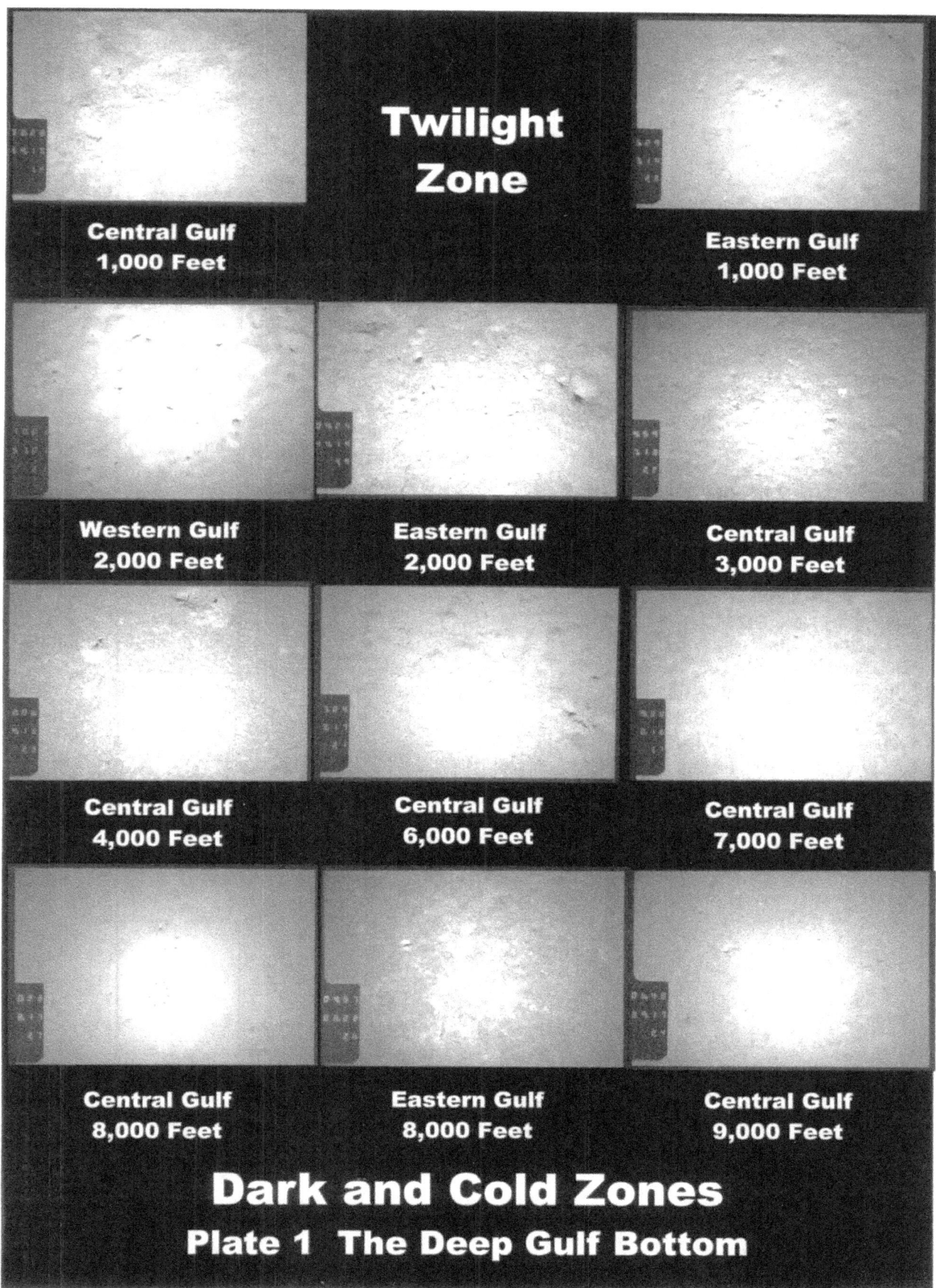

Twilight Zone

Central Gulf
1,000 Feet

Eastern Gulf
1,000 Feet

Western Gulf
2,000 Feet

Eastern Gulf
2,000 Feet

Central Gulf
3,000 Feet

Central Gulf
4,000 Feet

Central Gulf
6,000 Feet

Central Gulf
7,000 Feet

Central Gulf
8,000 Feet

Eastern Gulf
8,000 Feet

Central Gulf
9,000 Feet

Dark and Cold Zones

Plate 1 The Deep Gulf Bottom

Sand waves on the bottom show that, at some times and places, strong currents can occur in the deep Gulf.

of sand, silt, and clay comprising the mud.

The photographs also reflect a tranquil current environment, overall. However, strong currents can occur at some times and places, as indicated by cross-bedded ripple marks in the sediments. Additionally, some bottom photographs show small rocks and pebbles appearing to sit on pedestals above the bottom, indicating the fine sediments have been scoured from around them by currents. These instances, however, occur in only a few of the photographs. The vast majority of the photographs document a tranquil environment in which fine sediments accumulate.

The animals living in the bottom sediments of the deep Gulf (called infauna) are typically small, numerous, and diverse. How small are they? Well, one component called the "meiofauna" are those animals that pass through a 0.300 mm (one-hundredth of an inch) sieve but are retained on a 0.063 (about two-thousandths of an inch) sieve. That is small. The

other component is called the macrofauna ("large infauna"). These are the larger worms and other small invertebrates that are retained on the 0.300-mm sieve. While they are larger than one-hundredth of an inch, a dissecting microscope still has to be used to be able to see and pick them out of the sediment samples.

Overall, the abundance and biomass of these small "food packages" for larger animals decline with depth. For the larger component (the macrofauna), numbers decline less rapidly than biomass, suggesting that the size of the animals decreases with depth. Of interest, the biomass of the

meiofaunal component of the sediment-dwelling infauna rivaled or exceeded the biomass of the larger component, the macrofauna. This observation is not characteristic of many other deep-sea areas. The Gulf macrofauna are thus quite small as compared with many other deep-sea systems, especially at the deepest depths. This observation lends credence to the idea that, in comparison with other slope systems, food or energy availability in the Gulf may be especially low, thereby limiting population density levels.

The abundance of the macrofauna in the deep Gulf actually shows a peak in abundance at a depth of

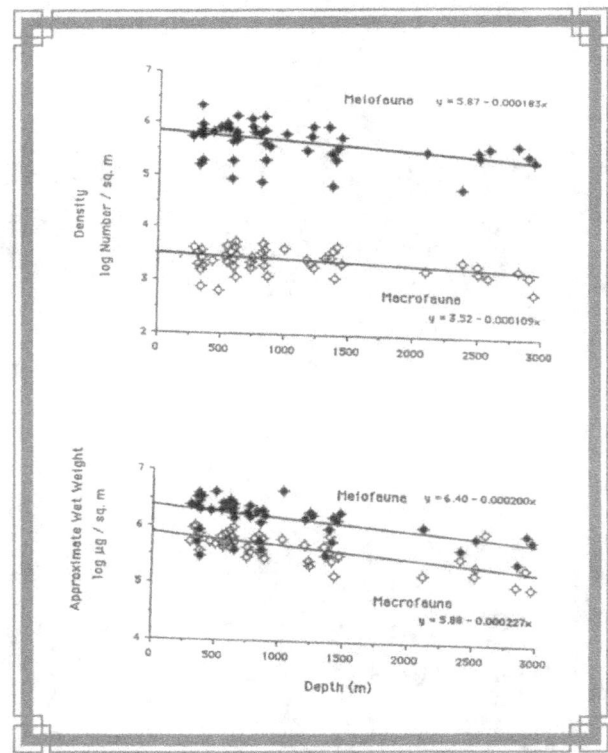

Relative number of macrofauna and meiofauna by depth (upper) and relative biomass by depth (lower). Macrofauna biomass declines more rapidly than numbers, indicating a decrease in size.

about 3,300 feet, and then declines as depth increases. Above this level, between 1,000 and 3,300 feet, abundance is higher than observed at the deepest depths, but lower than the mid-slope, high abundance peak seen at about 3,300 feet. We have learned above that a depth of about 3,300 feet is where the temperature reaches 4 °C and light disappears. Benthopelagic fish and invertebrates (the megafauna or "large fauna") will be shown to be much more abundant between 1,000- and 3,300-foot depths, than at deeper depths. Predation pressure may thus account for the lower standing stocks of infauna in the more shallow

zones of the Gulf slope above 3,300 feet.

Large Animals of the Deep Gulf

Deep-sea scientists classify animals large enough to be seen with the naked eye as "mega-fauna" (very large animals), even though they may be as small as one inch in length. These include everything from stalked, plant-like animals, to starfish, to shrimp and crabs, to fish. Characteristic assemblages of these animals are thought to be distributed in zones or bands extending across depth contours. However, there is much debate over how finely these bands can be defined; and, even if so, whether or not they are

biologically meaningful. They may simply be artifacts of sampling at discrete intervals along what is actually a continuum. Most all agree there is a meaningful break somewhere at about 3,300 feet, where light disappears and water temperatures become uniformly cold at about 4 °C.

On the slope at depths above 3,300 feet, there is, according to one school of thought, a single biological zone or continuum containing a "distinct shelf" fauna. Another school of thought subdivides this depth range into three parts with some rather exotic names: (1) the Shelf-Slope Transition Zone (median depth of about 1,000 feet with a total depth range

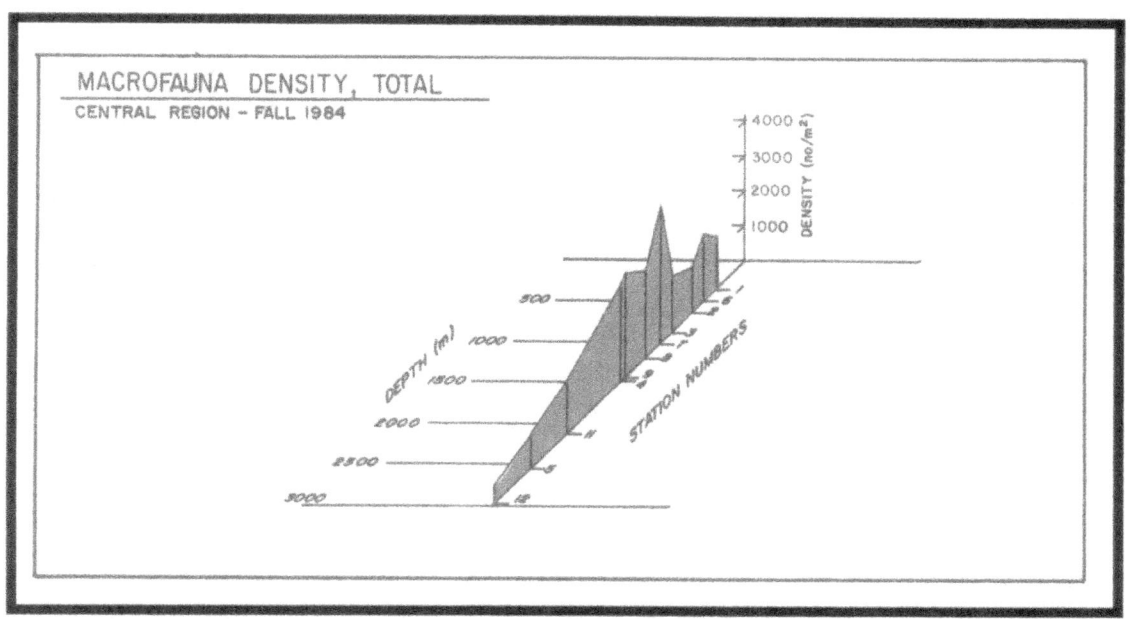

Macrofauna, food for larger animals, are most abundant at depths of about 3,300 feet (1,000 meters) and decline thereafter in direct association with depth increase. Reduced abundance above 3,300 feet may reflect predation pressure.

between about 500 and 1,500 feet); (2) the Archibenthal, Horizon A Zone (median depth of 2,000 feet, range from 1,500 to 2,500 feet); and (3) the Archibenthal, Horizon B Zone (median depth about 2,800 feet, range from 2,500 to about 3,100 feet).

Both schools of thought agree that between roughly 3,300 and 6,500 to 7,500 feet there is a broad depth range (called the Upper Abyssal Zone) of low megafaunal abundance and diversity containing a mix of animals characteristic of both deeper and shallower depths. Below 6,500 to 7,500 feet (the Mesoabyssal Zone), a true deep-sea fauna emerges, characterized by low abundance and a predominance of invertebrates. Whether there

are three or five biologically meaningful zones represented on the slope is not of importance for our discussion, or perhaps even for management purposes. Nevertheless, the five-zone naming scheme was used on the CD-ROM to organize the biota pictures, taken by the deep-sea camera, by depth. When reviewing these images, the reader will see that some species occur in several depth zones.

Trawls and Cameras— Different but Complementary

The bottom and near-bottom megafauna were sampled during the NGMCS study by using two fundamentally different but complementary techniques, bottom trawling and benthic photography. The trawl was

about 30 feet wide and was pulled along the bottom for about one hour at each location above 3,300 feet; and for two hours, more or less, at deeper sites. Overall, given the trawling speed, the trawl swept a bottom area of some 5 to 20 acres, depending on the depth being trawled. In contrast, the camera captured as many as 800 shots of the bottom at 8-second intervals over several miles, with each photograph averaging about 25 square feet. The total area photographed at a site would be on the order of 20,000 square feet, or less than one-half an acre. The area trawled is thus 10 to 40 times larger than the area photographed.

Because the area trawled was much larger than the area photographed, the trawl sample typically yielded a

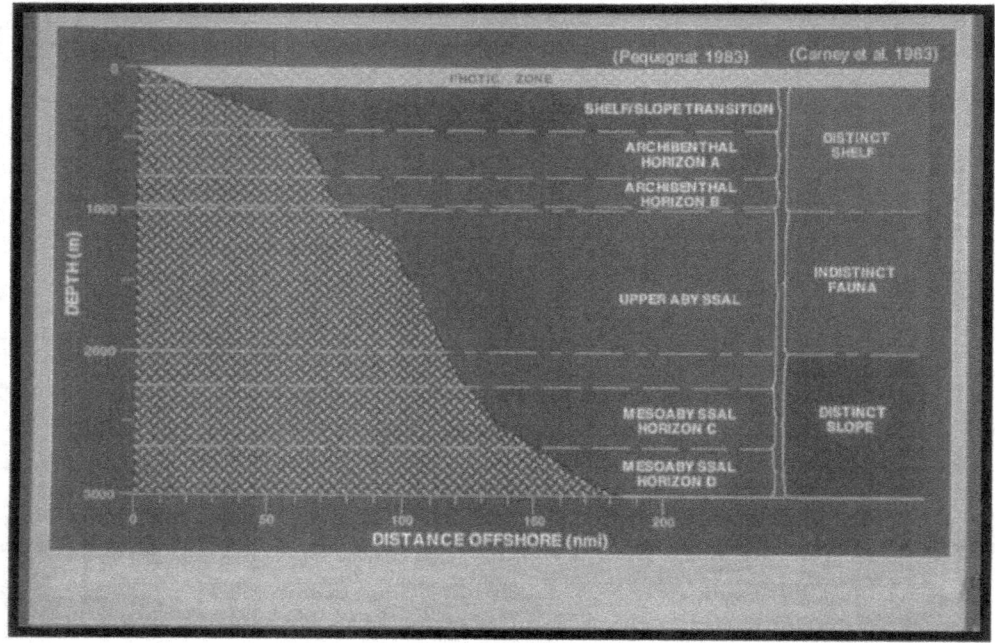

Opposing views of the zonation of faunal assemblages present at depth intervals down the Continental Slope.

A bottom trawl coming on board the research vessel as the deep-sea camera system awaits its turn to photograph the same depth zone.

larger number of specimens and species of large biota (for example, over 5,000 fish representing 126 species were trawled) than the benthic camera (488 fish were photographed, representing an unknown number of species). Comparisons of abundance must be based on some standardized area (like number per acre), but even then one must make many qualifying assumptions that are probably not true. For example, one must assume that the trawl will catch everything encountered equally well as is seen by the camera, which will see everything caught in trawls despite covering a much smaller area. Both methods have strong and weak points, and these must be taken into account in making direct comparisons. The methods are best viewed as complementing one another and this is the view we have taken in this essay.

Some 59 trawl tows were taken as part of the NGMCS study, yielding 5,400 specimens of 126 species of deep-sea fish, and over 30,689 invertebrates representing 432 species. The invertebrates in the trawl catches were more typically on the order of four to five times more numerous than fish, rather than about the eight times more numerous as is indicated by the total catches. Abundance of trawled megafauna was greatest on the upper slope down to 3,300 feet than at deeper depths, and higher in the eastern Gulf than in the western Gulf.

Both fish and invertebrate collections taken by trawling showed strong species dominance patterns; i.e., the overall patterns usually reflected the abundance of only one or two species. Only 22 of the 126 species of trawled fish

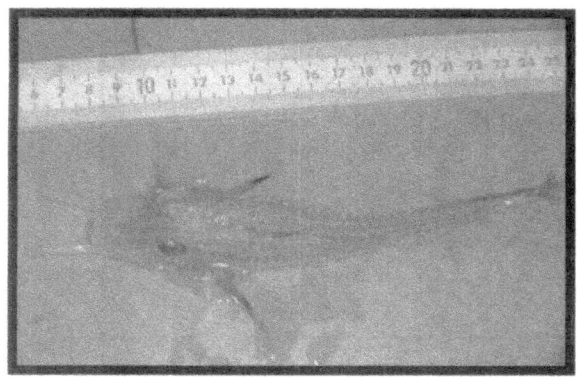
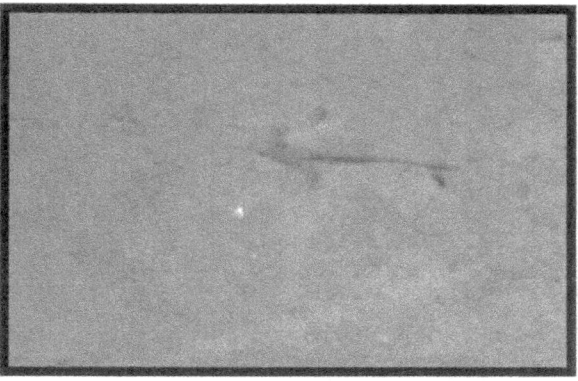

Observations taken by trawling and photography are complementary. The actual specimen (in this case, a sea robin) taken by trawling enables the collection of detailed size, weight, food and habitat data and accurate identification to species. The camera gives information about where these species live and their habitat.

had a total abundance of more than 1 percent of the total catch (more than 54 total specimens) and only 14 of the invertebrate species were represented by as many as 308 specimens (1% of the total)

Some 20,775 megafauna were counted in the analyzed photographs of the bottom and, for the most part, these could only be classified to major groups (e.g., sponges, sea pens, brittle stars, sea cucumbers, fish, etc.) rather than species. Nevertheless, no fewer than 190 species are believed to be represented. Invertebrates (20,287 specimens) were far more numerous than fish (488 specimens). However, one species each of a small sea cucumber and a chemosynthetic clam that were photographed (neither was taken in trawls) showed exceptionally high density, but only in a very small area. These two instances accounted for over half of the camera observations. If these are deleted from the camera samples for comparative purposes, 6,032 invertebrates were counted along with 488 fish. Invertebrates outnumbered fish in the photographs by a factor of 12. In the deep-sea Gulf, it

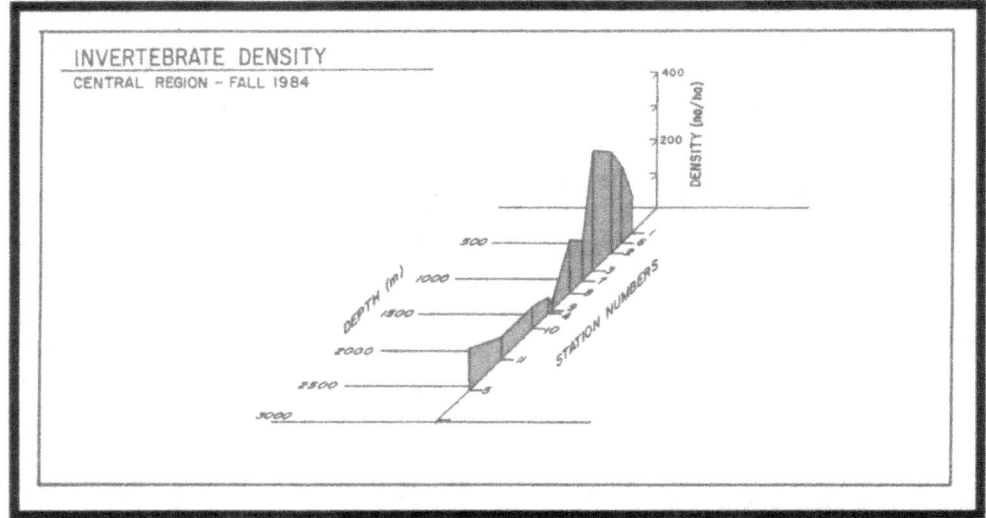

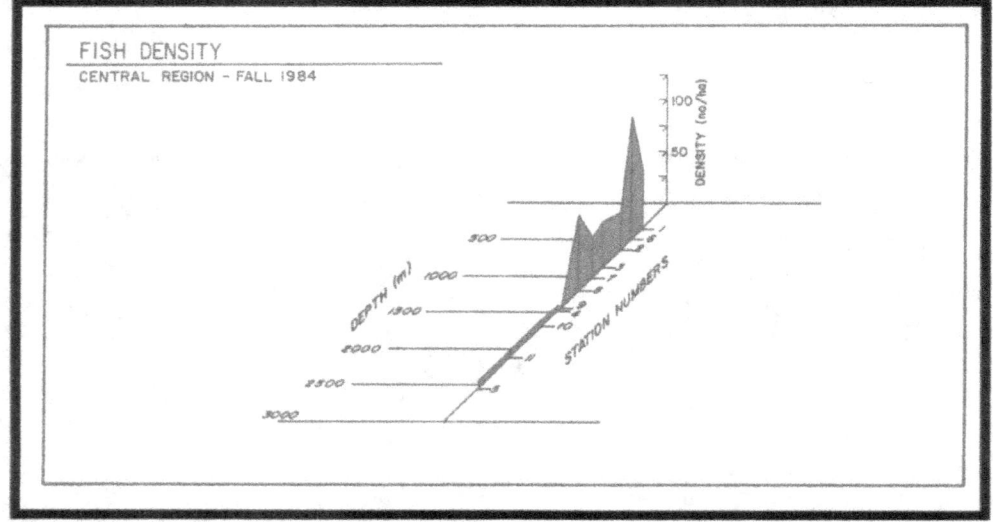

Abundance of megafaunal invertebrates (upper) and fish (lower) caught in trawls is higher in the shallower regions of the Continental Slope (generally above 3,300 feet) than in the deeper depths.

seems clear that invertebrates are more numerous than vertebrates (fish).

The trawl and camera observations exhibited similar patterns in abundance and diversity. The results of the benthic photography, with one exception, also showed abundance to be higher at depths above 3,300 feet than in deeper zones, and higher in the eastern Gulf than in the western Gulf. Thus, the two methods reflect overall agreement in general abundance trends.

As noted previously, the most abundant animal on the slope in the benthic photography sampling was a relatively small (about 1-inch long) sea cucumber called *Peniagone*. Over 11,000 of these small sea cucumbers were counted in the photographs. They were all seen on the central transect and most were observed in a very narrow depth range. The peak abundance occurred at a depth of about 4,000 feet. The very narrow depth and station distribution and their close proximity to a chemosynthetic community suggest an association. This, the most abundant of any organism documented by the photography, was not taken by trawling. Many animals in the deep sea are small, fragile forms not amenable to capture by trawls.

Look closely and you will see that this bottom is literally crawling with a small sea cucumber called Peniagone.

For comparison, the most abundant animal taken by trawling (3,393 specimens) was a small shrimp called the thread-footed shrimp (*Nematocarcinus rotundus*). This shrimp averaged about three-fourths of an inch long (maximum size was 1.2 inches) and was not identified in the benthic photography. It was taken in trawls on all cruises, all transects, and at nearly every station between depths of 1,600 and 3,300 feet. This shrimp averaged about the same size as the small sea cucumber, yet,

despite being big enough to see, was not documented in the benthic photographs. Thus, size alone does not account for the differences between what is seen with a camera and what is taken in a trawl. Patterns of aggregation (clumped versus scattered widely over a large area), sample sizes, and fragility of the animal are also important factors.

The second-most abundant animal seen by the camera was a bivalve or clam, now known to have been a chemosynthetic species. A very restricted high-density zone was encountered by chance at a single station (C7) on the central transect. None was collected by trawling despite the large area trawled.

The sea pens (*Alcyonaria*) were the third-most photographed megafaunal category, and species of sea pen ranked seventh in the

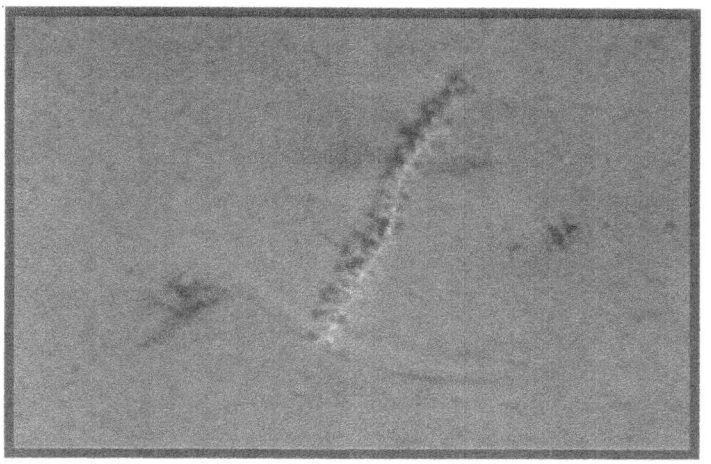

A graceful, sedentary sea pen waves above the bottom, filtering the water to obtain food in the energy-limited deep Gulf.

number of trawl-caught animals. Some 13 species of alcyonarians were taken in trawls. As a group, sea pens were found over the full range of depths sampled.

Deepwater shrimps and crabs comprised over 45 percent of the invertebrates captured by trawling and about 25 percent of the megafauna counted in the photographs. While different species individually showed different depth ranges of occurrence, overall abundance was highest at around 1,700 feet and abundance dropped dramatically below 3,300 feet as compared with shallower depths. Interestingly, densities (number per unit area) reflected by the trawl sampling were far lower than densities estimated by the photographs. The same was true for starfish and brittlestars (called asteroids and ophuiroids by scientists) and for fish.

Plate 2 shows photographs of some of the characteristic deep-sea invertebrates, including shrimp and crabs, delicate and not so delicate sponges, large sea cucumbers, anemones, squid, and other invertebrates of the deep Gulf. Likewise, Plate 3 shows characteristic forms of deep-sea fish including skates and rays, pancake batfish, rat tail fish, hakes and cod-like fish, gapers, and others. Many of the adaptations to the deep sea look bizarre to those familiar with sportsfish of the shallow Gulf. More examples of the deep-sea fauna are shown on the CD-ROM.

We reviewed all of the 48,000 photographs to compile Plates 1 and 2, selecting a representative photograph of each different animal we encountered. Not all photographs of each species were selected, just a representative one. Nevertheless, one cannot miss the observation that relatively few photographs contain any animal in view, and even fewer have more than one animal. With the few exceptions of dense aggregations, the animals are widely scattered—few and far between.

Another striking observation is that many of the fish photographs and some of the invertebrate photographs show an association with

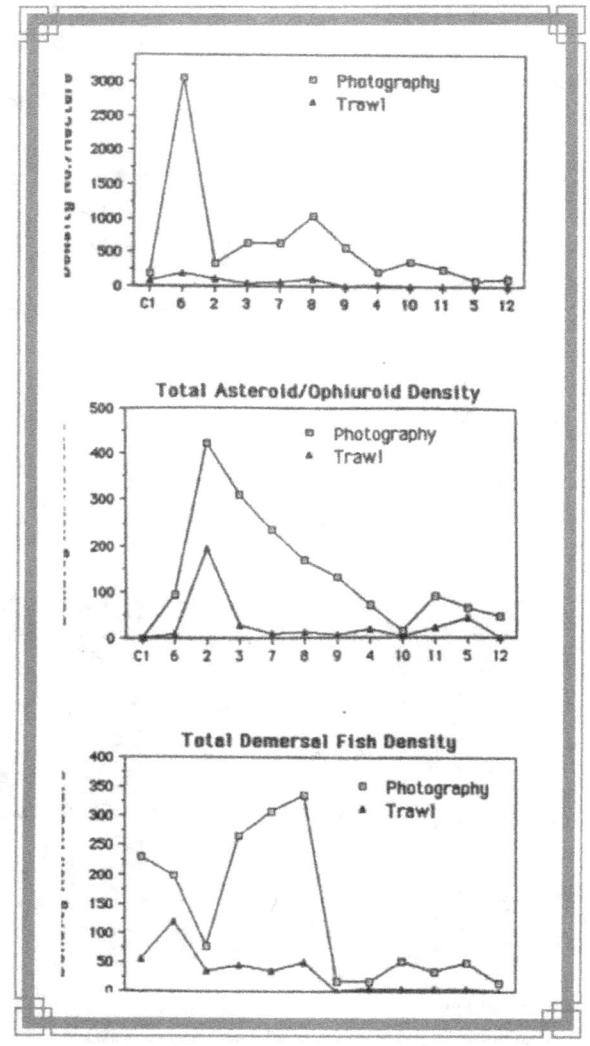

Comparative densities estimated by using cameras and trawls for shrimps and crabs (Decapods, top), starfishes (Asteroids/Ophiuroids, middle) and fish (bottom) from the top to the bottom of the Gulf Continental Slope.

Plate 2   Invertebrates of the Deep

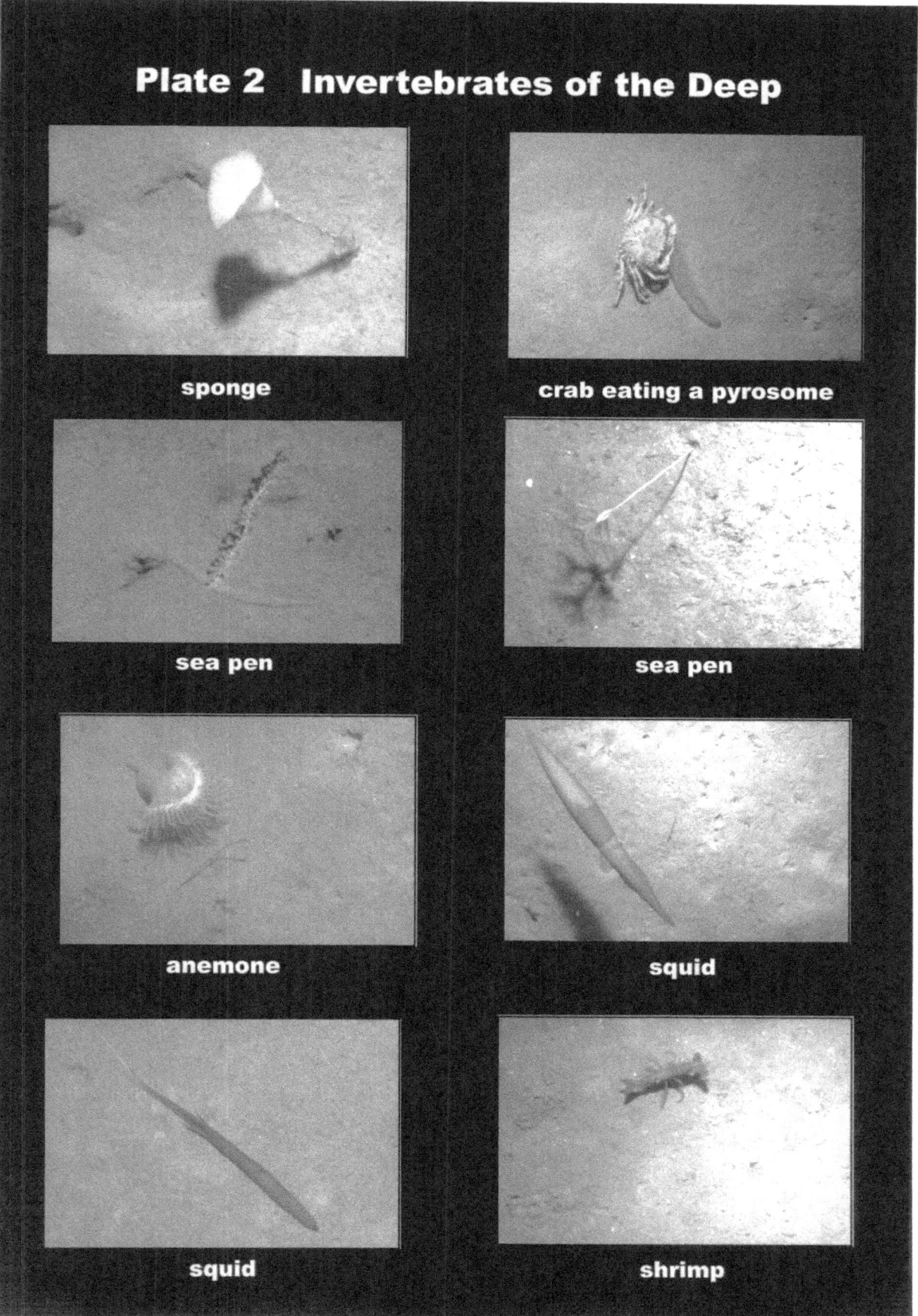

sponge

crab eating a pyrosome

sea pen

sea pen

anemone

squid

squid

shrimp

21

Plate 2 Invertebrates (continued)

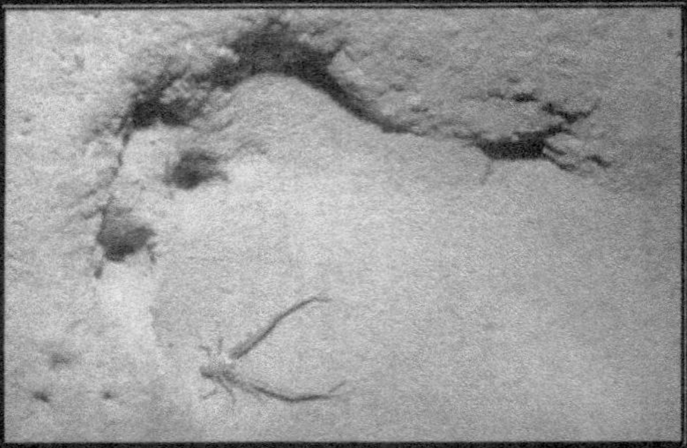

crab

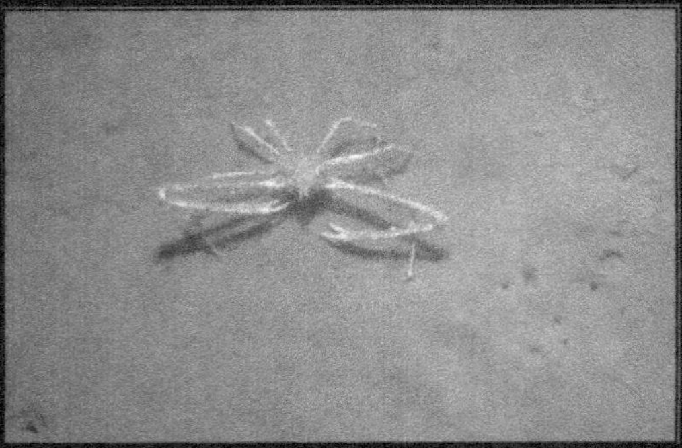

spider crab

crabs copulating

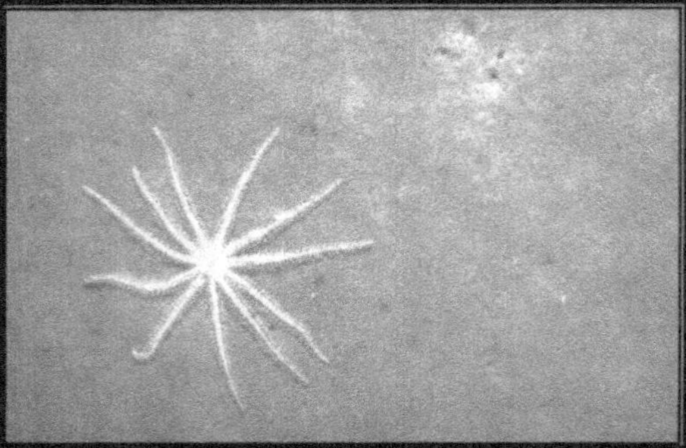

starfish

starfish

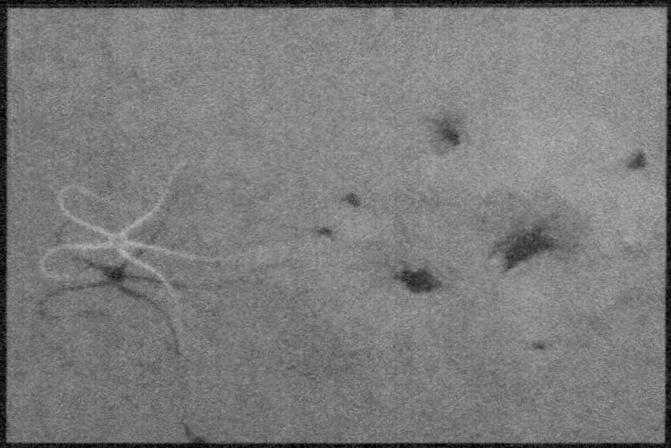

brittle star

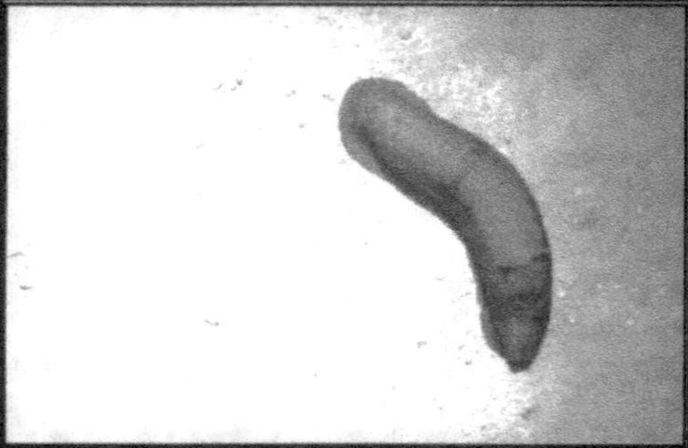

sea cucumber

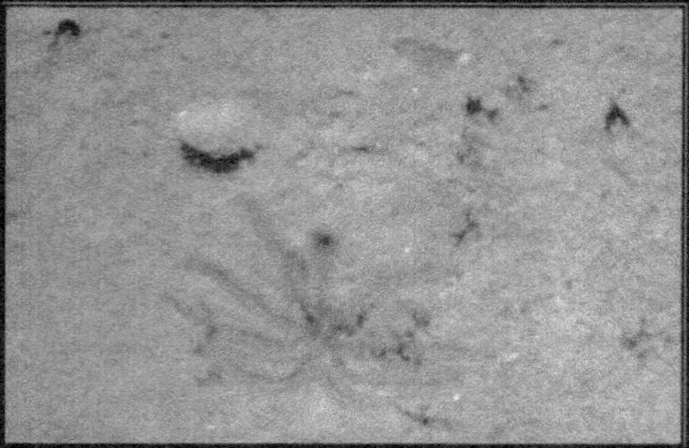

crinoid

Plate 3 Fishes of the Deep

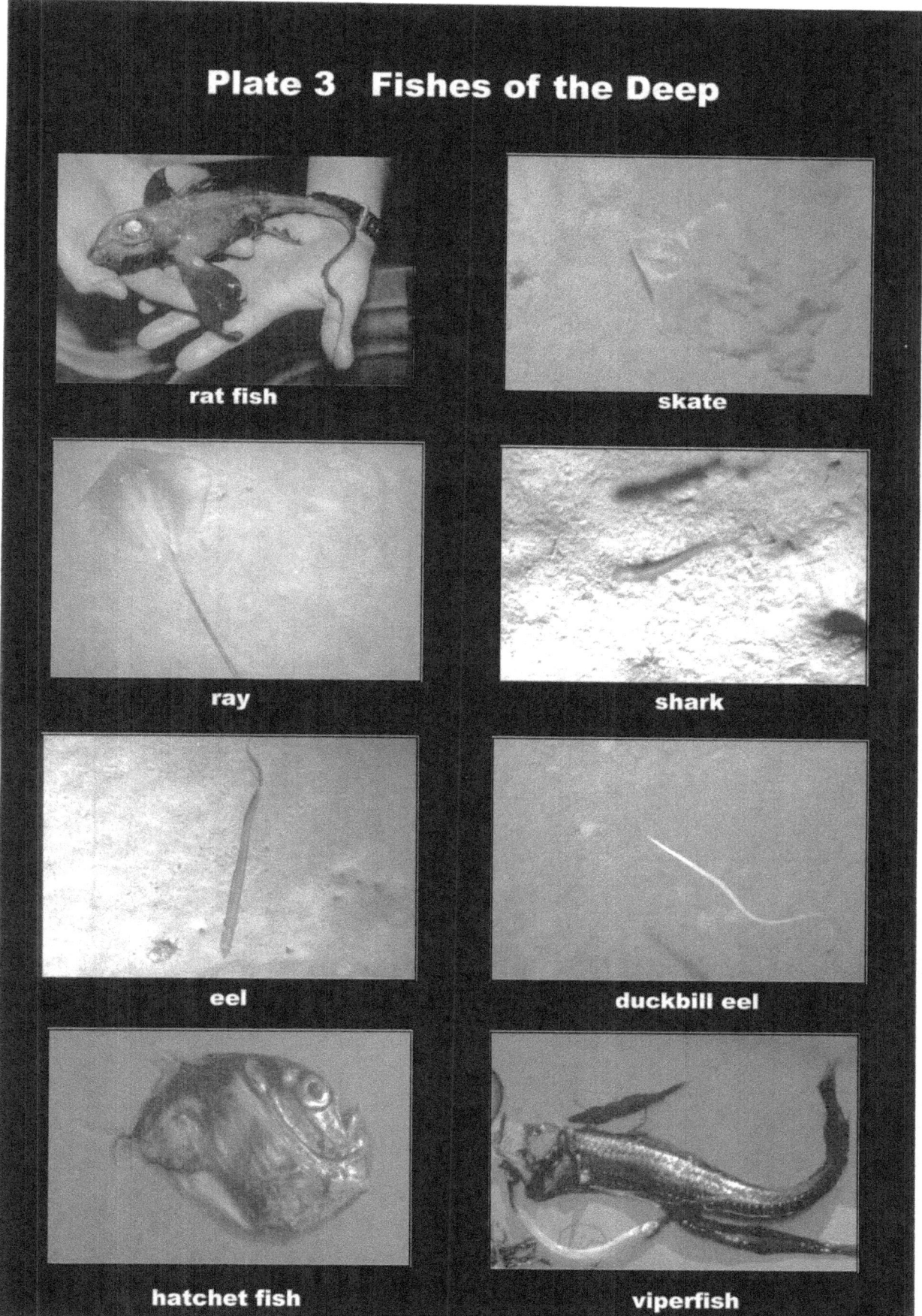

rat fish

skate

ray

shark

eel

duckbill eel

hatchet fish

viperfish

Plate 3 Fishes (continued)

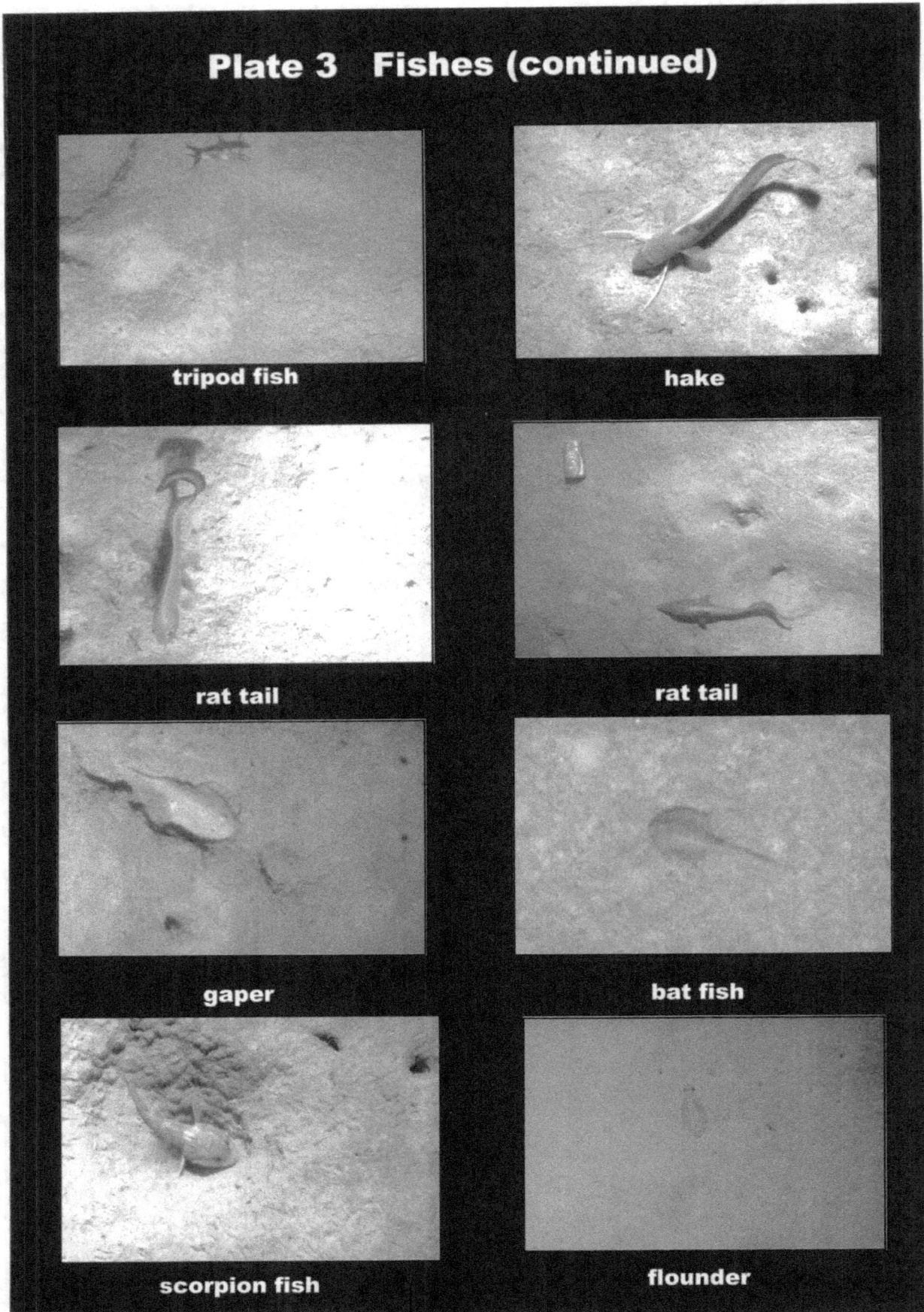

tripod fish

hake

rat tail

rat tail

gaper

bat fish

scorpion fish

flounder

some bottom irregularity like a rock or a hole. These structures likely offered cover or protection from predation, as well as represent sites where organic matter tends to accumulate. Such sites might be food-rich compared with surrounding soft bottoms—a good spot to feed if one eats detrital matter or a good spot to ambush those attracted to organic matter accumulations.

The physical appearance of the deep-sea fauna reflects adaptations for living under conditions of total or near total darkness, crushing pressure, generally weak currents, little food, cold, and on a featureless fine mud bottom. The animals are usually small and fragile, and are anatomically adapted for these severe conditions. The bulk of the animals in the deep Gulf eat by filtering the water, sweeping or eating the sediments, or scavenging the occasional dead fish, whale, or anything else organic that falls to the bottom.

DEEP-SEA OIL AND GAS DEVELOPMENT OBSERVATIONS

Deep-sea oil and gas development activities were beginning about the same time as the NGMCS study was being completed in the late 1980's.

Quantitative photography taken with a large, unmanned submersible remotely operated vehicle (ROV) is available from one of these developments, the BP Exploration, Inc. Pompano Project. This development proceeded with the drilling of 10 wells from 1992 to 1994 from a single-jacket (Pompano Phase I) at a depth of about 1,300 feet in MMS Lease Block Viosca Knoll 989.

Phase II began with the installation of a subsea template in about 1,900 feet of water four miles downslope in MMS Block Mississippi Canyon 28. Seven wells were drilled at this site between 1995 and

A deep-sea development showing drillship with ROV, subsea templates, and pipelines running up the slope to a standard production platform in shallower water.

1997, and one additional well was drilled in February-March 1998. The wells were drilled, in part, with nontoxic synthetic-based fluids (SBF's), some of which were discharged adhering to pulverized cuttings. These vegetable-based esters are highly biodegradable and may sus-tain bacterial activity at levels intense enough to cascade the effect upward in the food chain.

Sediment core samples and megafauna photographic surveys were taken in July 1997 around the subsea template, several months after the completion of the original seven wells drilled with the subsea template, and in February-March 1998, immediately following the drilling of the last well. The core samples showed remarkable densities of infauna as compared with the NGMCS study results. Even more surprising was the observation that high densities of megafauna (fish and invertebrates) were present around the subsea template. These organisms were seen in association with the structure of the template and the pipelines, and cruising over the rough bottom marked by large chunks of mud left by the riserless drilling phase that occurs at the start of drilling the well. All indications were that, at these depths, the structure afforded by the template, pipelines, and rough bottom has a reef effect, as has

Scorpion fish and crabs living in the structure provided by a subsea template.

Deep-sea crab perches on a pipeline.

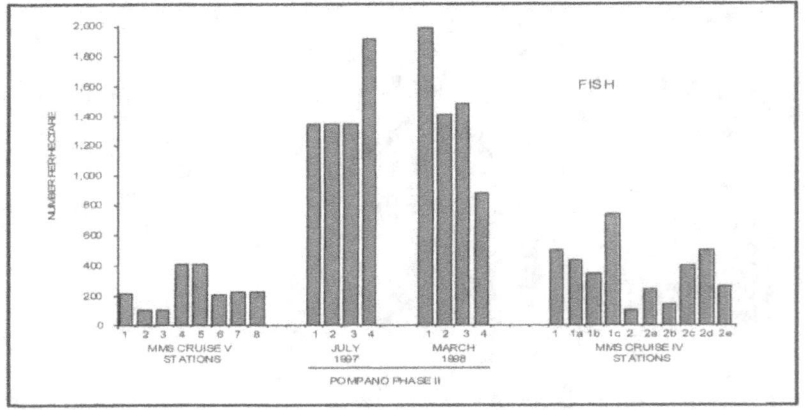

Estimated densities of demersal fish based upon photographic transects for the eastern and western Gulf of Mexico compared to estimates for Pompano Phase II video transects. See map at bottom of page 2 for MMS station locations.

been noted for shallow-water oil platforms.

THE PRESENT AND FUTURE

The NGMCS investigation provided the first synoptic view of an undeveloped deep Gulf of Mexico. Acceleration of deepwater oil and gas activities began in the mid-1990's. In 1997, MMS sponsored a Deepwater Workshop to determine if new deep-sea studies were needed to evaluate better the effects of deepwater developments. The participants endorsed the idea that new studies were needed. The need for updated information about the continental slope was echoed by attendees at contemporary MMS Information Transfer Meetings, who stressed that more also needed to be known about the abyssal plains of the deep Gulf basin at the base of the slope.

Thus, a new study, "The Northern Gulf of Mexico Continental Slope Habitats and Benthic Ecology Study," was funded by MMS and began in 1999. When it is completed, a comprehensive data and information base will be available that can be compared to the pre-development information base gathered by the Northern Gulf of Mexico Continental Slope Study.

Research Platforms for Deep-Sea Studies

Research Vessels

Manned Submersibles

Platforms and Unmanned Submersibles (ROV's)

27

REFERENCES

The complete findings of the Northern Gulf of Mexico Continental Slope Study can be found in four reports:

Gallaway, B.J., L.R. Martin, and R.L. Howard (Eds.). 1988. Northern Gulf of Mexico Continental Slope Study, Annual Report: Year 3. Vols. I-III. Annual Report to the Minerals Management Service, New Orleans, LA. Contract No. 14-120001-30212. OCS Study MMS 87-0059 through 87-0061. 1,490 pp.

Gallaway, B.J. (Ed.). 1988. Northern Gulf of Mexico Continental Slope Study, Final Report: Year 4. Vol. I: Executive Summary. Final report to the Minerals Management Service, New Orleans, LA. Contract No. 14-120001-30212. OCS Study MMS 88-0052. 69 pp.

Gallaway, B.J. (Ed.). 1988. Northern Gulf of Mexico Continental Slope Study, Final Report: Year 4. Vol. II: Synthesis Report. Final report to the Minerals Management Service, New Orleans, LA. Contract No. 14-120001-30212. OCS Study MMS 88-0053. 318 pp.

Gallaway, B.J. (Ed.). 1988. Northern Gulf of Mexico Continental Slope Study, Final Report: Year 4. Vol. III: Appendices. Final report to the Minerals Management Service, New Orleans, LA. Contract No. 14-120001-30212. OCS Study MMS 88-0054. 378 pp.

All photographs in this report and many more have been compiled on an indexed CD-ROM.

Both this report and the CD ROM are
available from

U.S. Department of the Interior
Minerals Management Service
Gulf of Mexico OCS Region
Public Information Office (MS 5034)
1201 Elmwood Park Boulevard
New Orleans, Louisiana 70123-2394
Telephone Numbers: (504) 736-2519
1-800-200-GULF

The Department of the Interior Mission

As the Nation's principal conservation agency, the Department of the Interior has responsibility for most of our nationally owned public lands and natural resources. This includes fostering sound use of our land and water resources; protecting our fish, wildlife, and biological diversity; preserving the environmental and cultural values of our national parks and historical places; and providing for the enjoyment of life through outdoor recreation. The Department assesses our energy and mineral resources and works to ensure that their development is in the best interests of all our people by encouraging stewardship and citizen participation in their care. The Department also has a major responsibility for American Indian reservation communities and for people who live in island territories under U.S. Administration.

The Minerals Management Service Mission

As a bureau of the Department of the Interior, the Minerals Management Service's (MMS) primary responsibilities are to manage the mineral resources located on the Nation's Outer Continental Shelf (OCS), collect revenue from the Federal OCS and onshore Federal and Indian lands, and distribute those revenues.

Moreover, in working to meet its responsibilities, the **Offshore Minerals Management Program** administers the OCS competitive leasing program and oversees the safe and environmentally sound exploration and production of our Nation's offshore natural gas, oil and other mineral resources. The MMS **Minerals Revenue Management** meets its responsibilities by ensuring the efficient, timely and accurate collection and disbursement of revenue from mineral leasing and production due to Indian tribes and allottees, States and the U.S. Treasury.

The MMS strives to fulfill its responsibilities through the general guiding principles of: (1) being responsive to the public's concerns and interests by maintaining a dialogue with all potentially affected parties and (2) carrying out its programs with an emphasis on working to enhance the quality of life for all Americans by lending MMS assistance and expertise to economic development and environmental protection.